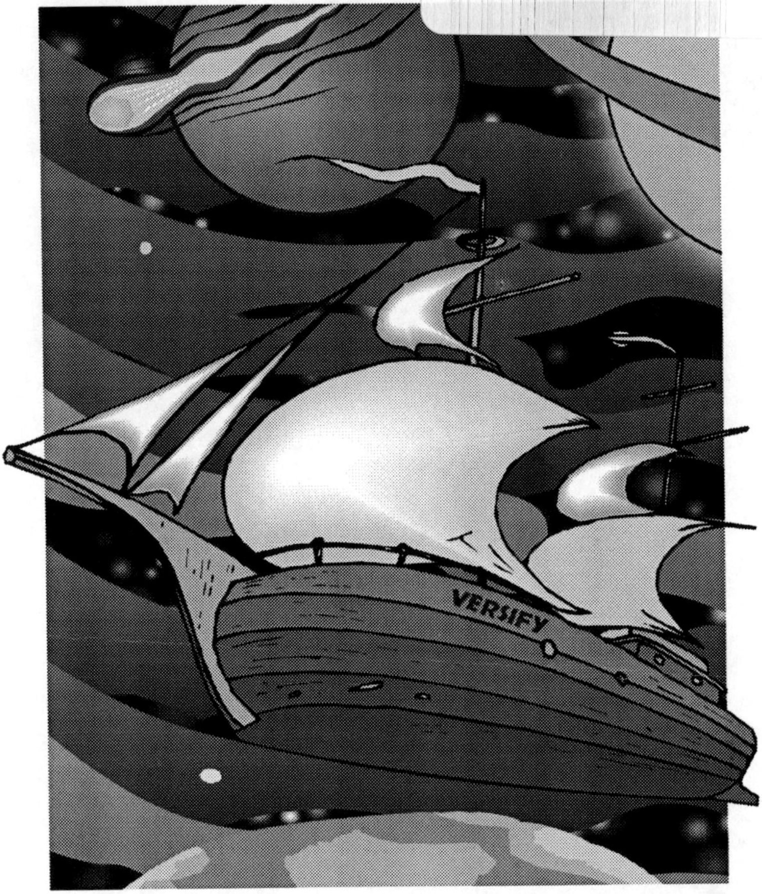

POETIC VOYAGES WILTSHIRE

Edited by Allison Dowse

First published in Great Britain in 2001 by
YOUNG WRITERS
Remus House,
Coltsfoot Drive,
Peterborough, PE2 9JX
Telephone (01733) 890066

HB ISBN 0 75433 316 7
SB ISBN 0 75433 317 5

FOREWORD

Young Writers was established in 1991 with the aim to promote creative writing in children, to make reading and writing poetry fun.

This year once again, proved to be a tremendous success with over 88,000 entries received nationwide.

The Poetic Voyages competition has shown us the high standard of work and effort that children are capable of today. It is a reflection of the teaching skills in schools, the enthusiasm and creativity they have injected into their pupils shines clearly within this anthology.

The task of selecting poems was therefore a difficult one but nevertheless, an enjoyable experience. We hope you are as pleased with the final selection in *Poetic Voyages Wiltshire* as we are.

CONTENTS

Nicholas Hedley-Harper	30
James Mulholland	31
Scott Lewis	31
Caitlin Skeates	32
Jamie McDougall	32
Kelly Mitchell	32
Laura King	33
Emily Whitcombe	33
Lauren Cundick	33
Natalie Chadwick	34
Sasha Gould	34

Holt VC Primary School

Lee Hulbert	34
David Lees	35
Lisa Harris	35
Charlotte White	35
Rebecca Vickery	36
Bethany Gibbons	36
Emma Harrison	37
Colleen Alcock	37
Laura-Jean Ramshaw	38
Fiona Wailes	38
Joshua Lynch	39
Lorna Estill	39
Emily Horrocks	40
Jason Gee	40
Samuel Vincent	41
Kirinji Kaur Rai	41
Michael Cranwell	42

Keevil CE Primary School

Katie Bell	42
Cameron Reid	43
Sam Breach	43
Christopher Barnes	44
Edward Breach	44
Sam Young	45

Pitton CE Primary School

Genevieve Cox	78
Stephanie Westcott	78

Preshute Parochial Primary School

Julie Smillie	79
Matthew Bond & William Hanson	80
Ethan Palmer	80
Rebecca Carter	81
Jennifer Asherson	81
Daniel Lowe	82
Rebecca Franczak	82

Roundstone Preparatory School

Laura Gumbley	83
Jack Pike	84
Robert Comba	84
Alice Baker	85
Sebastian Bates	86
Christian Cooper	86
Simon Carter	87
William Gibbs	88
Francesca Tucker	88
Jonathan Davies	89
Victoria Bingham	89

St John's Catholic Primary School, Trowbridge

Matthew Barlow	90
Maria Jones	91
Amanda Gardner	92
Hannah De Boorder	92
Ella O'Neill	93
Jennifer Corless	93
Michael Barlow	94
Andrea Ling	95
Abby Long	95

St John's CE Primary School, Warminster

Daniel Welling	96
Scott Sleeman	96
Kirsty Martin	97
Kelly McGrath	97
Jade Dewey	98
Stephanie Power	98
Gemma Pickin	99
Natalie Alexander	99
Victoria Gill	100
Stefan Burt	101
Katie Mae Symes	101

St Thomas À Becket CE Primary School, Salisbury

Lisa Edens	101
Colin Coleman & Adam Baker	102
Douglas Clifton	103
Matthew Charlton	104
Kate Young	104
Tess Carter & Tania Charlton	105
Josie Carter	106
Joshua Baker	107

Sutton Veny CE Primary School

Theo Knott	107
Sophie Orr	108
Gemma Sheppard	108
Katie Bunce	109
Sophie Arnold	109
Tansey Shingleton	110
Louis Frank	110
Verity Prior	111
Jonathan Ashley	111
Alex Drage	112
Sophie Hall	112
Charlies Chiola	113
Sam Marden	113

The Poems

BEANO WEBSITE

Postie, Postie, have a rest,
The Beano website is the best!

On the computer where everyone is,
Dennis the Menace has his own little sis.

Gnashing and gnipping are Gnasher and Gnipper
And Les Pretend is getting it all.

Biffo is a quiet lad,
Minnie the Minx is minxing mad.

Ivy the Terrible is a real feature,
The Bash Street Kids hate Teacher.

Calamity James has bad luck,
Roger the Dodger, dodges for a buck.

Ball Boy thinks his fouls are bad,
Crazy Daisy hates Ernest real bad.

Nathan Rainer (11)

THE UGLY TOAD

There's this person who lives down the road,
My friends call him the ugly toad when we ride past,
We think he's watching,
He has a black cat who sits on the chair,
When I looked in the cat disappeared into thin air.

My friends dared me to open the toad's gate,
It was too late!
He was watching,
He came outside and shouted at the top of his voice!
My friends ran off,
I was just standing there like he had put a curse on me.

The toad asked me if I would like to have some tea,
For some reason, I said 'Yes please,'
We had biscuits and cake but not
Just any cake but the best cake I have ever had
And one more thing he isn't the toad,
He is one of my friends!

Heidi Bawden (9)
Avondale School

CHRISTMAS

The Wisemen followed the golden star,
But Bethlehem is so far,
They bring precious gifts for baby Jesus,
Gold, Frankincense and Myrrh will please us.

But Christmas changes every year
And we exchange with our parents most dear,
We light the fire and then go to bed,
Some sherry for Santa and for Rudolf some bread.

Christmas Eve has finally left
And gone away has the theft,
We're going to have a really good time
And with our relatives drink some wine.

Alex Wilson (9)
Avondale School

THE CREATION

A piercing clang,
A big bang.

A planet called Mars,
A million stars.

A brand new moon,
A sun at noon.

An end to the dark,
A yellow spark.

A strange new life form,
A sparkling dawn.

A milky way,
A frosty day.

God's elation,
At his creation!

Ben Crisp (9)
Crockerton CE Primary School

UNICORN'S DREAM

In my mind, in my dreams, dashing in the
Green, green grass.
Were the strange shapes, it was unicorns!
They were stunning, sparkling with a touch of magic,
Their coats were like silk, they pranced over the moon.
Singing as they danced in harmony with the moon,
One was left behind - shy, cold, hurt he was
Shivering, suddenly there was another. I tried
To help but they snapped at me, and went off.

From that day on I haven't seen a unicorn,
So now I'm 92 and my dreams are more often
And I hope I don't have a long wait!

Jessica Wright (10)
Crockerton CE Primary School

DREAMING

In my thoughts and in my dreams,
I imagine I am an angel,
Floating high above the clouds,
Fluttering in the wind,
With my beautiful golden wings
I feel as if I am on top of the world
Until I awake,
I can't wait till the next night,
That is to live my dream again.

Sarah Williams (10)
Crockerton CE Primary School

THE WINTER ROBIN

Hopping in the snow
Puffing out his cherry breast
Pecking in the snow
Looking for some little worms,
Hiding in the winter snow.

Ella Kendal-Peel (8)
Crockerton CE Primary School

KITTEN CINQUAIN

Kitten
Soft and cuddly
He runs and chases me
He tumbles over his fun toys
He purrs.

Adam Smith (9)
Crockerton CE Primary School

ANIMALS HAIKU

A cute animal
Which is the best animal
I love animals.

Ella Halsey (9)
Crockerton CE Primary School

DIGGER

D igger, Digger, my little dog,
I n the garden playing behind the log,
G oing to the hosepipe, that's rolled in a ball,
G urgling the water, forming a waterfall,
E very day he digs and digs,
R unning around doing little jigs.

Emily Jones (9)
Crockerton CE Primary School

SPRING!

Spring is on the way,
There are flowers bursting with colour,
Also daffodils sway like ballerinas
As the breeze gently blows
Meanwhile baby birds fight for food.

Emily Scutt (10)
Crockerton CE Primary School

THE WOOF

A howl, a growl, a yip, a yelp,
Dalmatian puppies need our help,
A bark, a woof, a long bow wow,
Find our puppies, find them now.

Charlie Young (9)
Crockerton CE Primary School

SPIDER'S WEB

Glistening in the frost at the break of dawn,
A long thread of silk quivering in the breeze,
Sparkling in the sun like the remaining twinkle of starlight,
The ravenous spider lurking on double top,
Patiently waiting for an unlucky passer-by when . . .
Bullseye! . . .
The pulse of the web triggers the gleeful spider,
To scurry to its high score.

Oli Parry (10)
Crockerton CE Primary School

GHOSTS!

I sat in a corner shaking with fear
My eyes were red-raw full with a tear,
A gust of wind skimmed my back,
A white image appeared out of nowhere,
Was it a ghost?
I wasn't sure.

Amy Williams (10)
Crockerton CE Primary School

A YOUNG LADY FROM FRANCE

There was a young lady from France
Who loved to jiggle and prance
She danced to a tune
By the light of the moon
That graceful young lady from France.

Hannah Walters (11)
Crockerton CE Primary School

TROLL

A terrible troublesome tyrant troll with two heads,
Big as a six-storey building,
With greeny yellow skin covered with blood
As many weapons as a Swiss army knife,
All as devastatingly dangerous as each other!
Ready to rip and tear into an enemy's skin,
Piercing heavily,
Enemy of witches, wizards, dwarfs, elves and trolls
Lives in a big black cave.
Dug deeply in the menacing middle of dangerously dark wood!
Surrounded by white wasting-away bones!
A terrible two-headed troublesome tyrant troll!

Lloyd Jermy (11)
Crockerton CE Primary School

CAR FOR SALE

Scratched paintwork, dented keys,
Can be re-started with total ease,
Seats made of leather,
Good for all weather,
Bought in 1990, car shop in Bath,
People often walk by and laugh,
Inside an eight-person holder,
Engine will run even when older,
Needs a good owner, breaks down a bit,
Does anyone want to buy it?

Stefanie Young (11)
Crockerton CE Primary School

THE LAST VOYAGE

Floating, gliding, sailing fast,
Snow-white sails upon the mast.
Rolling waves hit the boat,
Fighting hard to keep afloat.
Looking out for other ships
Going on exciting trips.
When a ship comes sailing near,
All the crew are filled with fear,
Fire the cannon, raise your sword,
The other ship starts to board.
The battle continues all the day,
The ships start floating in the bay
And finally when they reach the land
Not even the captain is left to stand.
Both the ships have crumbled down
And still today they haven't been found.

Matthew Piper (10)
Crockerton CE Primary School

LIST POEMS

In a sailor's chest, I found a rugby sword,
Some gold and a dead fish.

In a mermaid's purse, I found a gold brush,
A pearl necklace and some earrings.

In an alien's pocket, I found an eyeball,
A map of Mars and a funny creature.

In a captain's beard, I found a sharp knife,
Some food and a pocket knife.

Felicity Webb (9)
Crockerton CE Primary School

CHIMPANZEE

A platform weaver,
A leaf receiver.

A nut breaker,
A fruit taker.

A knuckle walker,
A chattering talker.

A facial expressor
A memory possessor.

A family groomer,
A flea consumer.

A caring troop,
A friendly group.

Katie Davies (9)
Crockerton CE Primary School

A SLOBBERY TONGUE

A slobbery tongue,
A wagging tale.

Hair all curled up,
Just like a snail.

Rolling in the mud,
Running like mad.

A catalogue to make,
Me a dog!

Luke Tones (9)
Crockerton CE Primary School

THE STORM

Thunder bashing,
Lightning flashing,
Rain lashing,
Splashing, rushing,
Flooding.

Wind whistling
Through the house,
Bending trees,
Crashing, roaring,
Breaking everything.

Jordon Kirk (8)
Forest & Sandridge CE Primary School

THE STORM

Rain pitter-pattering,
Splashing,
Wind whispering,
Whistling,
Thunder crashing!
Lightning flashing!
Wind roaring,
Growling,
Rain pitter-pattering,
Splashing,
Wind whispering.

David Jones (8)
Forest & Sandridge CE Primary School

THE LEFT-OUT BOY

He was standing in the park
He had a sad face
No one to play with
He didn't like this place.

He was shaking wild
Now who wants to play with this child?

Folks played jokes on the boy
His eyes were weary
All of the bullies broke his toys
The bullies looked scary.

He was shaking wild,
Now who wants to play with this child?

He asked his dad to mend his toy,
This time he was going to defend it
The bullies crowded round the boy
The bullies were very fit.

He was shaking wild,
Now who wants to play with this child.

He was always on his own,
A sad life he leads,
A left out and lonely boy,
A friend is what he needs.

He was shaking wild
Now who wants to play with this child?

Steven Sims (9)
Forest & Sandridge CE Primary School

WHAT IT WOULD BE LIKE IN THE FUTURE?

What will be left here for me?
Will there be green grass?
Will we be able to go on holiday in space?
Nobody knows if everybody will have laptops?

Will it be safe to eat meat?
Will rivers become cleaner or dirtier?
I don't know does anyone know?
Will robots be doing everything for us?

Will more people build houses on flood plains?
Will factories' chemicals pollute the sea?
Does anyone care about the nature?
Have we destroyed nature in our world?

Richard Everett (8)
Forest & Sandridge CE Primary School

LIFE IN THE FUTURE

In the future will life be like it is now?
Will we still have to do our jobs or will robots do them for us?
Will we still go on holiday to Greece and Spain or will
we have space holidays?
Will there be more entertainment in our cars?
PlayStation, TV, hand-held computers for every child?
Flying cars in the sky?
Who knows what life will be like in the future?

Jessica Dobson (8)
Forest & Sandridge CE Primary School

POLLUTION

Why, why, why do we pollute this Earth?
Is there any need?
Is there any worth?

When will the forests and the fields be free?
When will there be no pollution in our seas?

Will the earth benefit if we walk?
Will e-mail take over our talk?

Let's make the Earth a better place
And give the environment a bit more space.

Let's try and stop polluting this Earth
Because there really is no worth.

Stephanie Parkin (9)
Forest & Sandridge CE Primary School

THE FUTURE

In the future,
Will we have space holidays
Or maybe hand held computers?

Will there be hover cars
So we can hover each day?
Could there be robots that help around the house?

Will we have TV in our cars,
To keep us all happy?
Will all this happen?

Toby Dagger (8)
Forest & Sandridge CE Primary School

METAPHORS FOR HARVEST

Fields are rough, green seas crashing over hedges.
Corn is a golden blanket, a rich treasure in the setting sun,
Stalks of wheat are slashing knives cutting the ground.

Trees wave sadly goodbye to the summer,
Their bare bones rattling dizzily in the wind.
Bronzed feathers fall from trees, swimming through the air.

Vegetables hide underground ready to pounce,
Potatoes are burrowing moles, digging down, nestling to keep warm,
Red apples are clowns' noses, children's rosy cheeks, glowing,
Bananas are happy smiles swinging from trees.

Morning frost is glittering jewels sprinkled on the grass.
Evening mist is acrobats twirling unseen through the sky,
Harvest is a generous gift given to us each year.

Class 5 (Ages 9-11)
Forest & Sandridge CE Primary School

SPACE

Chilly in the night,
Moon shining bright,
Twinkling in the sky,
Stars glowing up high,
Shadows like a dark shape moving,
The quiet is soothing,
The orange sun starts to rise
And the dark dies.

Fred Rogers (8)
Forest & Sandridge CE Primary School

THE STORM

A storm swept leaves
Off the trees.

The storm raised the seas,
The thunder was thumping,
Lightning was frightening,
Bumping,
Wind howling - growling,
Thunder was roaring,
Children screaming,
Grown-ups feeling sad.

Amy Bone (8)
Forest & Sandridge CE Primary School

THE STORM

One winter's morning,
There was a big flash of
Lightning!
All was sparkling,
Until the rain was pouring.
Thunder, lightning,
Crashing, crashing,
Rain lashing, lashing,
In the storm.

Stephanie Wilkes (8)
Forest & Sandridge CE Primary School

THE BLOWING RAIN

The rain is blowing,
It's thumping strongly at the door,
The wind is yelling at the rain,
It's tapping furiously at the window -
'He's trying to get me!'

The rain is crying into a huge puddle,
It sounds like he's clapping his hands,
Like he's pretending he's blind.
The rain is peeping in the door,
I told him to 'Go away' but he didn't.
He just waited until I came out,
I came out of my room,
He was gone, so I jumped up and down,
But he was still there looking up from the stairs,
I screamed, I looked out of the shredded torn window,
Outside it was grey.

Hannah Raddy (10)
Grafton CE Primary School

THE MOON

The moon is curved, the moon is round,
The moon is bright all through the night.

You can hear the howling foxes, you can hear the hedgehog,
The moon is bright and you can see all through the night.

The moon is a ball, the moon is big,
The moon shines crystal-gold,
The moon is bright, all through the night.

Matthew Smith (7)
Grafton CE Primary School

HORRORS OF IMAGINATION

Feeling uncomfortable you sit
But gliding silently here and there,
You hear the things that they do,
Beyond the horrors of your imagination.

Eyes are filled, blue, cold tears,
In your head you hear them,
Sobbing and screaming, they howl and shout,
Whimpering in the shadows.

In your head, you see them
Flickering in-between the light and dark,
Silencing your cry for help.

John Palmer (10)
Grafton CE Primary School

RABBIT

A rabbit is friendly,
Rabbits are nice and fluffy.

They can jump,
They are big,
They like people,
They like vegetables,
They like playing.

I love rabbits.

Harriet Lewis (8)
Grafton CE Primary School

WATER

Water is good for you,
Water is dangerous,
When the sun shines on the water, I feel happy all day long,
Water is sparkly when the sun smiles on it.

I swim in the water, it feels smooth in the sunlight,
It's wavy and won't stay still,
It plays with you and races with you,
The wind pushes it away in waves.

Water can be as calm and sensible as children,
But it can be noisy and rough.

Chloe Hawkins (7)
Grafton CE Primary School

WATER

The water is still and calm,
Yet sometimes is dangerous,
It feels cool as we have fun in summertime.

It is blue pain, dribbling down your hand
And sparkling diamonds jumping up and down,
Playing hide and seek with the sun.

Wind chases the water into waves,
It is strong to push the boats away.
But water is fresh to drink and good for you,
The water is still and calm.

Rosie Lewis (8)
Grafton CE Primary School

WIND

The wind is kicking the leaves about,
It is pinching air with a bang,
Whistling impatiently at the window.

The wind comes out to play
Nobody wants to play or be his friend,
So the wind goes home very sad.

I go outside and the wind is there,
I ask him to come in,
He keeps blowing the cover off me,
He comes and has tea with us.

Kelly Hawkins (10)
Grafton CE Primary School

CATS

Cats asleep anywhere,
On the table, on the chair.

Sleeping silently in a ragged cardboard box,
Or in the huge cupboard,
With your favourite frocks.

Sleeping on the window sill,
Waiting patiently for their next meal,
Sleeping here and sleeping there,
Cats can sleep anywhere.

Kerrie Black (10)
Grafton CE Primary School

THUNDER

Thunder sparks, the thunder thumps,
The thunder makes loud noises,
It creaks,
It crunches and bumps and punches
And makes big lumps all over my body.

The thunder rumbles like an empty stomach,
The thunder is like a block of crystal gold,
If you try to escape you will discover a bolt,
If you jump in a puddle you will be surrounded by wires,
If you are going home, watch out for the thunder.

Dominic Finch (9)
Grafton CE Primary School

WHAT IS IT?

White as a ghost,
Sharp pointy teeth like daggers
Shoot in your neck,
Looking for something to drink.
Eyes like cannon balls,
Blood dripping from his mouth,
His cloak swinging everywhere he goes,
Creeping about at night,
He pounces on you with a fright,
You're dead!
It's a vampire!

Lucy Stuart (9)
Heytesbury CE Primary School

FIREWORKS

The bonfire gobbles up Guy Fawkes,
Flying its fiery head around.
Laughing.

Getting moodier now,
Wants to play.
It pops!

Red and green fists,
Fighting through the air,
Shouts and shouts.

Dancing through the air,
Waving its arms around,
Until the music stops.

Getting sleepy,
Had its fun,
Falls asleep.

The soft smell of smoke fills the air,
He whispers,
I'll be back . . .

Sophie Anderson (9)
Heytesbury CE Primary School

THE BLACK AND WHITE BIRD

They are like a submarine,
Their head like a cockpit,
Their tails like a rubber,
Their body the hull,
Blunt, but deadly beak, is yellow,
Their muddy, white belly fur gets darker as it sinks into the water.

As fast as an underwater rocket,
Still lurking for fish,
It sees one,
Full steam ahead,
It dodges a rock,
The penguin grabs the fish.

William Davies (10)
Heytesbury CE Primary School

CATS

Brown, black and white,
Sleeping all day in the rain,
Sometimes they can be a pain.

Jumping on tables,
Never seem able to stay still.

Rolling around in their sleep,
Even though they are sleek.

Rolling around,
Falling on the ground,
Love human company,
Even in Germany.

Long tails swishing,
Soft paws padding.

Their little nose sniffing,
Silky fur soft.

Cats, cats, cats.

Abbie Hale (10)
Heytesbury CE Primary School

MY OWN BLACK STALLION

I love the sound of its piercing voice,
The shape of its head fills me with magic,
The way it rears up, before it gallops along.

Where does it live? I hear you ask,
A long way away, on the moors of Scotland,
It reigns over others with no competition.

Just to see its jet-black coat, fills me with instant pleasure,
The sound of its beating hooves across the sand,
                    just leaves me with wonder.
The way it moves swiftly over the hills without hesitation.

What does it feel like? You ask me now.
It feels soft and gentle, delicate and silky.
The way it leads, shows in an instant, just how wild it is.

I feel its gorgeous velvet nose,
Just shows how lucky I am.
I love its loyalty to me,
The way its tail and mane flows against the wind.

Just what is this animal?
Your last question is,
With its flowing mane and tail
And jet-black coat,
My own black stallion.

Kayleigh McDougall (10)
Heytesbury CE Primary School

EAGLE

Flies round in circles to get food,
Lives on mountains with its babies,
Glides in the air all day,
Getting rare in the world,
A massive animal.

Beautiful,
Incredible eyesight,
Eats nearly anything,
Brown and white,
It's an eagle.

Luke Windsor (9)
Heytesbury CE Primary School

THE VULTURE

Swiftly swooping,
Gladly gliding,
Never stopping,
Smelling death.
It's found its prey,
Gliding round the dying ox.
The ox fell dead,
Diving down on its prey,
Tearing open the skin,
Pulling out the meat,
It's the vulture.

Storm Harland (10)
Heytesbury CE Primary School

SNOWY

Snowy is white, brown, black,
Snowy is small and hairy as can be.
Rushing around all the time,
Eating apples, carrots, cabbage, celery,
Busy Snowy, silly Snowy.

Heather Newman (7)
Heytesbury CE Primary School

STORM PARTY

Wind whistling,
Mixed with thunder clashing in the sky,
Rain furiously drumming.

Tiles sliding off the roof,
Grabbing on with all their might,
First they smash then more move.

Rain drumming on the windows,
Making a tune as it goes along,
Some were doing the limbo.

Thunder and lightning were having a
Party in the sky,
With the dim yellow light,
Then the party starts to die.

Lots of music gone away,
As the sun rises and birds begin tweeting
And up starts the day.

Ashlie Heal (10)
Heytesbury CE Primary School

THE CAT

The sun is going down,
The cat is scratching at the door,
It's time to come in,
It's dinner time.
The bowl is tipping on the floor,
A glint of a sparkle.

Time to go outside,
This is the life of a cat.

Kirstie Sturmey (10)
Heytesbury CE Primary School

MY HAMSTER

My hamster is the best,
Better than all the rest.
She scrambles in her cage,
Six weeks is her age.
She likes to run in her ball,
And she's not allowed in the hall.
But best of all, she is cute.

She eats green vegetables and carrots,
Nibbles is better than a parrot!
Hamsters come out at night,
But they don't come out when it's light.
She's got very small eyes,
And she's not allowed to eat pies.
But best of all, she is CUTE!!!

Samantha Grindley (9)
Heytesbury CE Primary School

DO YOU KNOW IT?

A drooly mouth pounds about,
Digs his claws into the fat little cat.
Gulps his tea in a flash,
Soppy as a kitten,
Barks for England!
Tail swishes side to side,
Ears flapping up and down,
Nose sniffing out the enemy,
Fur scratching along the way,
Silly old dog!

Sam Baggs (10)
Heytesbury CE Primary School

It's A Cat

Silky black fur,
With a wild man's purr.

Beady eyes,
Can tell no lies.

Sharp claws,
Buttoned up paws.

Shiny nose,
Has no toes.

Pointy ears,
Whiskers like spears.

Long tail,
Curls like a snail.

Begins with a 'C'
Ends with a 'T'

It's a cat.

Emily Howlett (9)
Heytesbury CE Primary School

My Cat

My cat is the best,
She's better than all the rest.
She purrs,
She sleeps,
She eats.
That's why she is best.
There are all kinds of pets,
But for me, cats are the best.

Sarah Chapman (8)
Heytesbury CE Primary School

SOMETHING OR SOMETHINK?

Swiftly moves through the house,
Eyes glaring, seeking, shining,
Beautiful coat glistening in the sun,
Razor-sharp teeth waiting . . .
Paws grabbing tensely,
Silky head moving,
Paws slowly going thud, thud, thud,
Sleeps like a stone . . .

Sarah Darby (9)
Heytesbury CE Primary School

THE ELEPHANT

Long, swaying trunk,
Small peering currant eyes.
Charging through,
Pulling down the trees that are in the way.
Friendly wild giant,
Grey wrinkled skin,
Legs making a mini earthquake with every step,
African or Asian.

Rosemary Cross (10)
Heytesbury CE Primary School

THE BABY FOX

A baby fox has just been born.
His mother goes to get some corn.
He skips around till it's dawn,
Every day and all night long.

Emily Schofield (8)
Heytesbury CE Primary School

GLOW THE FIREFLY

To show you the way to play,
Look for my light and I'll show you the way.
We're about to go to the park,
And you can see me in the dark.

I have two blue eyes and one red nose,
And all day I sit on a rose.
At night I fly about,
And I'm allowed to shout.

So my life is brilliant and I love being a firefly.

Sophie Harbinson (9)
Heytesbury CE Primary School

GERBIL

Its little razor-sharp teeth,
Its white, silky-smooth fur and tail.

Its little claws like daggers,
Its small, pink nose,
Its little bony legs.

Its cute pinky-grey tongue,
Its bright-red eyes as quick as lightning.

And it is ten times faster than a white rat!

Charlie Comer (10)
Heytesbury CE Primary School

RABBIT

Jumping triumphantly through the vegetable patch,
Scurrying stealthily with a perfect match,
Fidgeting furiously to make a great catch,
Swiftly and powerfully, leaping to grab a big latch.

Watching the moon in a starlit sky,
Silky fur the colour of silver snow,
Eye darting around the night sky, on a quest,
Pointy ears like spikes,
It can only be the rabbit.

Nicholas Hedley-Harper (10)
Heytesbury CE Primary School

SOMETHING . . .

It jumps madly out of its cage, landing on the Lego box,
Leaping, dodging his master's grappling hands,
With happiness, heading for the food,
Scampers into the cupboard, taking four favourite peanuts with joy,
Claws the dressing gown and climbs up,
Dives under the duvet, makes a bed and starts eating.

Crafty and clever is the rat!

James Mulholland (9)
Heytesbury CE Primary School

FOOTBALL

All boys like football,
Taking corners,
Taking penalties,
Taking free kicks.
Passing,
Scoring,
We don't care.
We just like having a good time
With our friends.

Scott Lewis (8)
Heytesbury CE Primary School

MY TREAT

The zoo is fun
   Watching many unusual animals
      And me eating my iced bun.
         Elephants, monkeys, flamingos
            And much, much more.
               The zoo is fun
                  If I get my treat
                     To eat my iced bun.

Caitlin Skeates (9)
Heytesbury CE Primary School

BASKETBALL

You pass the ball,
You bounce the ball,
You dribble the ball,
   You tackle each other.
      You shoot,
         You score,
            You miss.
               That's what you do in basketball!

Jamie McDougall (8)
Heytesbury CE Primary School

GUINEA PIGS

Guinea pigs like hugs,
Guinea pigs like their cages cleaned out.
Guinea pigs like kisses,
Guinea pigs like a run to play in.

Kelly Mitchell (7)
Heytesbury CE Primary School

DOG AND CAT

The dog eats dog biscuits,
The cat eats beef.
The dog sleeps in a brown basket,
The cat sleeps on the bed.
The cat was playing with her ball,
The dog was chasing another cat!
They are friends.

Laura King (7)
Heytesbury CE Primary School

FAIRIES

I love fairies,
They fly in and out through the wind.
I would look after one,
If it had a bad wing.
I dream about fairies at night,
I would be sad if they had a fight
   Tonight!

Emily Whitcombe (7)
Heytesbury CE Primary School

PETS

Pets are lovely and cute,
Pets are furry and gentle too.
Sometimes smelly,
But still so cute.
Some like the night,
Some like the light.

Lauren Cundick (9)
Heytesbury CE Primary School

MY BEST FRIEND

My friend is my dog.
He is pleased to see me.
I cuddle him, I play with him.
He is my friend.
He loves me,
He comes and meets me.
I take him on a walk,
He talks to me.
He is my *best* friend.

Natalie Chadwick (8)
Heytesbury CE Primary School

HAMSTERS

Hamsters run around a lot all night long.
Hamsters eat grain and oat seeds.
Some hamsters bite.
Hamsters like cuddles a lot.
Hamsters play too.
Hamsters have to go in cages.

Sasha Gould (9)
Heytesbury CE Primary School

MARS

Mars is called the red planet, uninhabited,
People say that it's very dark but red,
The pink sky is very light,
It lights up the day.
The dry planet looks out at Earth,
I think people may live on Mars.

Lee Hulbert (9)
Holt VC Primary School

JUPITER

The big ball of swirling gas reflecting solar light
The massive storm always at its height.
Ringed red uninhabited
Spherical freezing and enormous.
We do not know much about it
And we cannot be on it.

David Lees (11)
Holt VC Primary School

PLUTO

Cold, dark, icy,
Pluto, alone on its own,
He doesn't like to be all alone.
Pluto, staring up in space while circling,
At a very slow pace.
He looks down to see blood-red Mars
Also circling at a very slow pace.

Lisa Harris (10)
Holt VC Primary School

MERCURY

This very tiny planet,
Lots of people like it a lot
Spotted and dotted all around,
It doesn't make a single sound.
This grey tiny planet
Cold and hot.
It travels round the sun
It doesn't stop.

Charlotte White (9)
Holt VC Primary School

THE SOLAR SYSTEM

The sun: glowing and fiery.
          Mercury: arid and very rocky.
Venus: dry but very gaseous.
          Earth: windy, lunar and humid.
Mars: dusty, rouge and volcanic.
          Jupiter: icy and barren.
Saturn: airless and glowing.
          Uranus: ringed, rocky and blue.
Neptune: the eighth planet from the sun.
          Pluto: small, icy, the last.
    But is it?

Rebecca Vickery (11)
Holt VC Primary School

THE SUN

The sun is a big round ball,
Its bright orange fiery flames
Are big, hot and gassy,
It's so awesome,
Scientists think it's classy,
It is distant and molten,
In its own way,
It's a bright yellow, reddy star,
It reflects very far,
We couldn't live without the sun,
I think it's shaped like a bun.

Bethany Gibbons (9)
Holt VC Primary School

NEPTUNE

Neptune is cold and icy,
Neptune is big and bare,
Neptune has no life forms living there,
Neptune!

Neptune is glossy and round,
Neptune is ocean blue
Neptune has tinges of frothy white too,
Neptune!

Neptune is serene and tranquil,
Neptune's spin is graceful,
Neptune is calming and peaceful
Neptune!

Neptune is desolate and elegant,
Neptune is mysterious,
Yes mysterious Neptune!

Emma Harrison (10)
Holt VC Primary School

PLUTO

Pluto is a small planet,
As small as small can be,
It is too cold for anyone,
And that includes me.
Pluto is a slow planet,
He takes his time
And if he was in a race,
He'd be last in line.

Colleen Alcock (11)
Holt VC Primary School

VISIT PLUTO

Pluto is a tiny ball,
Small and bright,
You can't see it at night,
It looks like it's white,
But it really is blue,
Grey mist circles Pluto,
Pluto is gassy,
Chalky and pale,
It looks quite frail,
But really it's not,
It's made of rock,
Pluto is dusty,
Like Mars,
But not rusty.

Laura-Jean Ramshaw (9)
Holt VC Primary School

SATURN

Saturn with its famous rings,
And its sixteen moons,
Saturn is a gassy planet,
With a layer of ice around it,
Saturn is multicoloured,
With stripes all around,
Including all the rainbow colours
And a couple more.

Fiona Wailes (9)
Holt VC Primary School

PLUTO

Pluto is icy,
Freezing,
Orbiting the distant
Solar system,
A chilly and slippery surface.
The smallest planet of them all.
It's grim,
Gloomy
Unfriendly in the dark,
Dim sky
The outermost planet
From the sun
Sad and unwelcoming.
Mysterious
Unknown
Bleak as the coldest winter's night.
No life
Sad
A ball of freezing ice
Circling the huge sun.

Joshua Lynch (11)
Holt VC Primary School

THE EARTH

Earth big and solid
It's blue and green
Earth spinning around
Like a spinning top
Tiny little us living on this planet.

Lorna Estill (9)
Holt VC Primary School

JUPITER

A very large gassy planet
Full of fluid
Speedy
Strong
Colourful
Bright

That is Jupiter

Jupiter's fast
Jupiter's metallic
Jupiter's massive
Jupiter's magnetic

Jupiter, the biggest planet

Stormy
Cloudy
Frosty
Freezing
Cold
Icy
Windy
I wonder if that is really
Jupiter?

Emily Horrocks (9)
Holt VC Primary School

JUPITER

Jupiter's big and round,
it is the biggest of all,
It is very far away,
Jupiter is colourful.

Jupiter's got sixteen moons.
that is why it's bright,
Jupiter is famous,
It lights up at night.

Jason Gee (9)
Holt VC Primary School

OUR SOLAR SYSTEM

From the boiling sun
To the tiny Pluto
From the mystical Mars
To the amazing Jupiter
Freezing on Neptune
It's incredibly hot on Mercury
Could there be life on Mars?
Saturn is showing off its beautiful rings
Astronomers look at distant Uranus
Are there any other planets out there?

Samuel Vincent (11)
Holt VC Primary School

MY VISIT TO MARS

The surface feels rusty,
It looks a bit dusty,
I see some dried riverbeds,
Mars looks like it's dead,
It feels like powder,
Slushy by lava,
I see some movement,
What could it be?

Kirinji Kaur Rai (9)
Holt VC Primary School

JUPITER

Very large Jupiter
Red and spotty.
Glowing in the dark
Shining on the Earth
Very large Jupiter
Covered in gas.
This colourful planet
Can be seen from Earth
Its big red spot
Can be seen from miles around.
This big planet is very stormy while
It's streaking round the sun
With its big large spot.

Michael Cranwell (9)
Holt VC Primary School

CAT

I think a cat
Should sit on my lap
Their ears are pointed
Their faces are round
The only thing they make
Is a sound
Their tongues are pink
Their teeth are small
If they walk about at night
You can't see them at all
But I think a cat
Should really sit on my lap.

Katie Bell (10)
Keevil CE Primary School

BIG BANG

B is for the bright explosion
I is for the large icy rocks that flew out
G is for the great volcano that erupted

B is for in the beginning
A is for the enormous animals that once lived
N is for the nasty dinosaurs that ruled the Earth
G is for the Galaxy we live in.

Cameron Reid (10)
Keevil CE Primary School

KENNING

A dirt flattener,
A dirt disturber,
A straw maker,
A grass cutter,
A muck scooper,
A weed killer,
A trench digger,
A dirt hauler,
A food mixer,
A maize cutter,

Put them together and
What have you got?

Farm machinery!

Sam Breach (10)
Keevil CE Primary School

A MATHS KENNING

A sum killer
A sum confuser

A problem harder
A problem solver

A brain twister
A brain teaser

A head filler
A head thinker

An odd multiplier
An odd puzzler

An even divider
An odd remainder

What am I?

Multiplication.

Christopher Barnes (11)
Keevil CE Primary School

KENNING POEM

A chicken eater.
A prey searcher.

A bullet escaper.
A night traveller.

A fast runner.
A dog father.

A den sleeper.
A big sniffer.

An excellent jumper.
A hole digger.

Put these together - what do you get?
A fox!

Edward Breach (9)
Keevil CE Primary School

FOOTBALL BOOT

A ball-smacker,
A foot-breaker,

A net-breaker,
A bar-shaker,

A ground-mover,
A turf-groover,

A stud-ripper,
A blood-ripper,

A lace-tripper,
A wet-whipper,

A worm-killer,
A dirt-filler.

What am I? A football boot.

Sam Young (10)
Keevil CE Primary School

THE MILKY WAY

I went to the Milky Way,
One peaceful summer's day.

It was all white and slimy,
And very untidy.

I visited all the stars,
And went way past Mars.

Until we came to a halt,
At an engine fault.

I woke up with a jolt,
And undid the bathroom bolt.

I pushed open the bathroom door,
And picked up my toothbrush of the floor.

Emer Hutton (10)
Keevil CE Primary School

YUCK AND YUM
(In honour of my very special Aunty Alice)

I can't bear custard,
I couldn't eat a plum,
Peas are just disgusting,
But chocolate is yum!

I hate curry,
I can't stand duck pâté,
Apples are yuck,
But chocolate's OK!

If you eat squid you're *mad,*
If you like broccoli you're *insane,*
But if you don't like chocolate,
You're out of your picking brain!

They say it makes you fat,
If you eat it ten times a day,
I say 'Go hang,
And pass the Milk Tray!'

Gus Collins (10)
Keevil CE Primary School

CAT!

A bad biter
A good fighter

A brilliant climber
An excellent chaser

A bird killer
A rabbit scarer

A naughty stealer
A little teaser

A dangerous scratcher
A tickly licker

Put these together I'm a cat!

Samantha Page (10)
Keevil CE Primary School

SNOW, SNOW!

Snow, snow
Before it goes,
Jump in it,
Shovel it and
Very, very quickly
Mould it!

Snow, snow
Before it goes,
Roll in it,
Steal it and
Very very quickly,
Ball it!

Snow, snow
Before it goes,
Throw it,
Kick it and
Very, very quickly
Lick it!

Snow, snow
When it goes,
It's snow good
Being sad.

Tom Coyer (10)
Keevil CE Primary School

KENNING

A long survivor
A smelly stinker

A little biter
A big eater

A small squeaker
A tiny stepper

A dainty sleeper
A fast runner

A sly sneaker
A quiet hunter

Put these together
I'm a hamster!

Emma Winney (10)
Keevil CE Primary School

SNOWBALLS

Snowballs die in many ways,
but no one seems to care these days.
We're made to lie upon the ground,
although we never make a sound.
We end up scattered across the floor,
or squashed under the garage door.
So the government has a pit fall,
no snowball welfare - that's all.

Edward Lund (10)
Kingsbury Hill House School

WAR

Soldiers walking into the gloom,
Soldiers walking to their doom.
Where they go is no-man's-land,
Barren Earth; no sun, no sand.
Families forgotten, death is what they fear,
Shells, the messengers of death, they hear.

The barbed wire fence,
Our last defence.
The rifle's ready,
Hold it steady.
Screams of death,
I lose my breath.
Though most don't survive
I'm still alive.

James Papworth-Smith (10)
Kingsbury Hill House School

SOLDIERS

Soldiers marching down the lane,
Towards utter hatred and bane.
Sounds of battle, noises of war,
Awful fighting and horrible gore.
Lots of killing, lots of dying,
Overhead the bombers are flying.

Soldiers marching down the lane,
It's not their fault, they're not to blame.
Dreadful feelings, miserable thoughts,
War is cold, war is fraught.
Huge explosions, loud booms,
Soldiers running to their dooms.

John Gibson (10)
Kingsbury Hill House School

SOUNDS OF WAR

There's a still silence hovering over the battlefield
'Rifles ready!' ends the uneasy quietness and the fear to move.
The raised arm hits the ground.
We charge and all hell is let loose.

We charge, guns blaze, explosions echo everywhere.
Innocent people killed brutally all around us.
Scared men's voices shouting for help,
Brave men carrying the injured on their back, to safety.

When the guns stop there's another eerie silence.
Then you hear groans of the injured
And cries of soldiers finding their comrades dead.
Then it starts all over again when a single shot is fired.

Joshua Eldridge (11)
Kingsbury Hill House School

WINTER

Short days, long nights,
Telly in the evening.
Outside the frost bites;
Breathing on windows
Lying on the ground
Resting on the branches. No sound.

Warm scarves, woolly hats
Thick gloves and fleecy coats.
Above the roof the chimney smokes
By the door huge coal sacks.
Hot soup crusty bread,
Hot water bottles warming my bed.

Thomas Wakelam (10)
Kingsbury Hill House School

A WINTER GARDEN

The grass was glittering like a flat mirror ball,
It made the garden look much less small.
The sun pushing out through a white cloud,
A robin chirping up a beautiful chorus, loud.
Cold air pushing snow down,
Through the atmosphere onto the ground.

The ground was white as white could be,
As far as you could see.
The winter months went on and on, December, January.
The berries started to come,
The snowmen died,
The flowers popped into view,
The white turned to green;
Soon it was June.

Morgan Taylor (11)
Kingsbury Hill House School

SNOWBALL

Once I was a tiny flake,
then I settled on the grass.
Little child comes to play,
scoops me up to make a ball.
Rolls me on and on,
until I am huge, white,
hard as a cannon ball.
Hurls me at another child,
Now I'm back; a flake again.

Stratford Canning (11)
Kingsbury Hill House School

THE COLD OF WAR

We soldiers have to march all day,
Into the sun and into the rain.
We have no choice to come or go,
This is war as most of us know.

We sing a song as we march along;
A jolly one to make us laugh.
This does not numb or hide our pain,
For we are here to kill and not to smirk.

When we think of our families,
We feel sad and low.
No one to comfort or shield,
Only the cold of war!

Georgia Wawman (11)
Kingsbury Hill House School

WINTER SONG

In winter there's a loud noise,
It sings a loud song.
It has such a rainy sound,
Moaning through the town.
The apples in the orchard
Tumble from their tree.
It's such a cold feeling,
It makes your spine quiver.
Yet, when indoors I feel so warm,
I still hear whistles loud and low.
The garden gate shakes
And climbs the garden wall.
Yet, when I shout 'Who's out there?'
It's nobody at all.

Christopher Williams (10)
Kingsbury Hill House School

THE GERMAN

I killed a German yesterday,
He gave a yelp
And straight away
I felt the guilt
And I felt his pain -
I realised he was dead!

He might've had a family,
He might've had a child.
So, I just killed a father
And now I feel quite wild.
Do others feel like I do
Or have I just gone mad?
All I know is I killed him,
And for that I feel really bad.

Joe Kelly (10)
Kingsbury Hill House School

WARTIME

Barbed wire everywhere,
All the soldiers in despair.
Bodies scattered all around,
An end to this battle needs to be found.
A new commander comes onto the scene,
The men think he's the best leader that's ever been.
Their spirits, hope and morale rise,
Now ready to give the enemy a surprise.

The men's luck is about to change,
As the bombers turn their targets to flames.
Also the artillery fire shells,
To which fire engines ring bells.
The noise of the battle reaches its height,
The soldiers know their cause is right.

Simon Pearson (11)
Kingsbury Hill House School

WINTER

Wake up to the silence,
Snow up on the ground.
Go outside I go and play,
Don't let the fun drain away.

Sledging down the hillside,
It's all fun and play,
Snowball fights and snowmen,
The fires and the fun.

Wake up and what has happened?
Where is all the fun?
Seems like all the snowmen
Just got up to run.

Vicky Grove (10)
Kingsbury Hill House School

A TREE'S WINTER

Branches bare and frosted over;
Buds in their coats and ready for spring;
The branches form skeletons blowing in the wind;
Trees feeling lonely without their leaves
Creaking and shrieking on a windy day
On the odd occasion it snows
The trees stand ramrod stiff under snowy coats.

Robert Oliver Vincent (11)
Kingsbury Hill House School

MILO THE DOG

Milo is so cool
He sits around and drools

All I say is true
He jumped up and he flew

He lived with an old man for two and a half years
He was very unhappy and he shed lots of tears

All the food he got was the size of a tin
That he found in a dustbin

He had a very happy face
When he came in with his suitcase

I take him for a walk
I'm trying to make him talk.

Alex Davis (8)
La Retraite Swan School

ALL DIFFERENT THINGS

Earth is in space
And it's God whom we grace.

We all have different voices
We don't have a choice.

When it's cold we wear a cloak
In the bath is where we soak.

The old man is wise
It wasn't a surprise.

It's money we earn
The sun makes us burn.

For parties we invite
We party all through the night.

Billy Hillyard (8)
La Retraite Swan School

SNOW

It is creamy and soft.
It is thin and thick.
It trembles from the rooftops.
It's cold and white.
It is very slidy.
It falls from the sky.
It makes the wind change instantly.
It is snow.

Mike Hollingbery (8)
La Retraite Swan School

SNOW

Snow snow every day making people happy,
Wonderful snowflakes
Landing on my head,
Like little dots going fast going slow,
Up and down,
Small and big.

Nice and soft, nice and white,
And nice and cold,
I hope it doesn't melt,
Falling with style
And flying like birds.

Perminder Tanday (7)
La Retraite Swan School

OUT OF SPACE

Up in space all planets lay
All round the year as well as May.
The Earth keeps going round the sun,
It doesn't sound like any fun.
Do aliens live on planet Mars?
Maybe even drive cars.
I wonder if aliens do exist,
In another galaxy in the mist.
The stars make a lot of shapes,
Most of them are lions or apes.
There is a ring round planet Saturn
It's really just a rocky pattern.

Chris McNulty (8)
La Retraite Swan School

A WINTER POEM

It's cold it's icy, Santa come soon,
Or it'll be so cold he must really zoom.

Suddenly I heard this thud I looked around
Then I heard these tiny pattering sounds

Then I fell asleep
Dreaming about toys piled deep

I woke early that morning to see my mum and dad
When I found out about no toys, I was sad.

Ben Morrison (8)
La Retraite Swan School

WINTER

When I see snow
From my bedroom window
Outside I go.

It is cold
I feel old
Snow I hold.

I build a snowman
Put a hat on him I can
Out of the garden I ran.

David Street (9)
La Retraite Swan School

BONFIRE NIGHT

F   ires are alight
I   llumination
R   ockets going up and banging in the bright night sky
E   choing fireworks
W hirling noise
O   ver crowds
R   eaching fireworks spurting colours
K   ite fireworks banging in the night light
S   izzling gunpowder banging then going out.

Josh Voce (8)
La Retraite Swan School

WINTER POEM

The ground is so hard the snow begins to fall
People make snowmen the wind is really cold.
Ponds are frozen, roads are slippery
No leaves are on the trees, lots of grit is on the road.
Snow on houses people skiing.

Matthew Garratt (9)
La Retraite Swan School

IT'S SNOWING

It's snowing, let's go outside
And make a snowball slide
Go whizzing down the playground
Having snowball fights
And making snow angels at night.

Kit Hobday (8)
La Retraite Swan School

WINTER POEM

The cloudy white snowflakes fall to the ground
Softly softly without a sound
I get on my sleigh
The horses in the field go neigh
The pond freezes
The winter wind breezes
The more and more snow falls
It is white at the top of every wall.

Lucas Griffiths (8)
La Retraite Swan School

AUTUMN

Falling flowing down they go
Bonfire night burning branches.

Hallowe'en with spooky faces
People sweeping up the leaves.

Windy weather blowing leaves
Children playing in leaves.

Thomas Mouland (9)
La Retraite Swan School

HOT AIR BALLOON

Hot air balloon
Hot air balloon
Let your sandbags fly.
Hot air balloon
Hot air balloon
Sailing through the sky.

Jonathan Dollittle (7)
La Retraite Swan School

THE FAIR

The fair is fun and frightening,
The sizzler is very exciting,
I like the candyfloss they sell,
And the very small golden train bell.

The coconut shy is great fun,
I bought three balls to throw and won!
The fishing games were very easy,
But the rollercoaster made me queasy.

Matthew Troup (9)
La Retraite Swan School

BONFIRE NIGHT

Bonfire night is fun,
Lots of people come.
Fires are burning,
Catherine wheels are turning.

Rockets go off with a loud bang,
Blue, red, yellow and lots more.
Glowing sparks in the night,
I cannot wait until Sunday.

Ryan Jackson (9)
La Retraite Swan School

WINTER POEM

Snow is glittering on the ground,
The flower buds are coming
Snowdrops, crocuses, scillas, irises
Are all their buds form the Earth.

Ice is sparkling on the pond,
The winter birds are coming
Blue tits, blackbirds, thrushes, goldfinches
Are all planning their nests in the trees.

Sam Lelliott (8)
La Retraite Swan School

CHRISTMAS POEM

Christmas is fun,
We laugh and run,
We open our presents,
Then we are done,

Christmas is bright,
Because of our lights,
We are singing our carols
On Christmas night.

William Thomas (9)
La Retraite Swan School

WINTER

It was a very snowy day
When I saw a person in a sleigh
He was big and fat
And best of all that
He was covered in snow all the way.

He would wait till the end of the day
Till he would come down the chimney
And say 'Merry Christmas, hey hey.'

Andrew Hall (8)
La Retraite Swan School

A WINTER POEM

I woke up once on a winter's day,
And asked the inventor 'What shall we play?'
The inventor said with a huff and a puff
'We will build a snow machine so rough!'
So we built it up, by the stove were the cats
And the machine used some rats
And so I had fun on the hills
On with the machine and out came thrills.

Timothy Brockbank (9)
La Retraite Swan School

A CATERPILLAR'S LIFE

The small, hairy caterpillar
Starts his journey today.

He wriggles and wriggles,
All of the way.

Under a full moon,
He slowly makes his cocoon.

The days and days pass,
While he waits in the grass.

One bright day he awakes,
He has to escape.

Oh! What a sight,
The pretty butterfly is in flight.

How lovely to be free,
And fly from tree to tree.

Ami Lynn Cranham (8)
Lowbourne Junior School

THE LOST RABBIT

There was a rabbit who lived in a cage,
And he was of a very old age.
One fine, sunny, lovely day,
He decided he would run away!
He dug a hole right under the gate
And ran down the road at a very fast rate.
A car zoomed past and gave him a fright,
Then he suddenly came to a cat then he did fight.
He decided being free wasn't much fun,
So he turned back around and started to run.
Never again would he ever roam,
Because there is really no place like home.

Kelly Singer (8)
Lowbourne Junior School

THE MERMAID'S JOURNEY

U nder the sea it's calm and peaceful
N osy fishes stop and stare
D aring dolphins dart around
E legantly I swim by
R aggy coral swaying and swishing

T he seaweed grabs me as I swim by
H oping to find the lost shipwreck
E vening draws near

S ea growls dark and gloomy
E ventually, sadly I turn back
A ll hope lost till next time.

Katie Sibley (8)
Lowbourne Junior School

YOU!

You!
Your legs are like lamp posts
You!
Your arms are like drumsticks
You!
Your belly is like jelly
You!
Your lips are like rats' tails
You!
Your eyes are like spinny Catherine wheels
You!
Your hair is like spaghetti
You!
Your tongue is like a snake
You!
Your neck is like a giraffe.

Hayley Fitzpatrick (9)
Lowbourne Junior School

A VOYAGE TO SPACE

I was in my spaceship
On the way up to the moon
I passed several planets
I hope I get there soon.

It's very dark at the moment,
Although the stars are sparkling.
I am stood by the window, looking out
All I can see is little green men
Larking about.

Daniel Turk (8)
Lowbourne Junior School

WE ARE GOING TO THE ZOO

On the journey in the car
We had to go very far.
We were going to the zoo
My friend was allowed to come too.
There were lots of different animals to see
From a penguin to a chimpanzee.
The sun was shining very bright
Everything felt just right.
We had a ride on the train
Oh no it's started to rain.
Mum brought us lots of treats
And an ice cream too.
Oh what a wonderful day we spent at the zoo.

Jordan Lukas (9)
Lowbourne Junior School

A RABBIT WITH A HABIT

There once was a rabbit
Who developed a habit
Of twitching the end of his nose
He sat on a hill in a striking pose
Then along came a man with a bullet in his gun
All the other rabbits shouted 'Run run run!'
His bullet hit the rabbit's limb
And that was the end of him.

Rebecca Emery (9)
Lowbourne Junior School

MY MIXED UP JOURNEY

I was driving in the car a fish ran past my window.
Looking out of the aeroplane window
I spotted a flying snake.
Floating along in the boat I had to rub my eyes
A kangaroo swam past me.
In a jeep in the jungle a lion hopped in front of me
And I had to try to skid to miss it.
Up up and away in a hot air balloon
I spied a bird prowling past me.

I was only going to the shop!

James Dark (9)
Lowbourne Junior School

IN SPACE IN A ROCKET

I am floating through space, past Mars
The red planet is shining as I go
There are little green things dotting about
'Who are they?' I asked myself
'Get my camera out!' I said, *snap!*
Oh 'yes' back to Earth!

Look! Look! at what I saw
Wow! That means there is life on Mars,
That will be worth a million pounds.

Liam Williams (8)
Lowbourne Junior School

LIONS

L   ions are fierce
I   n and out hiding
O   n and on they go
N   ow they have stopped
S   o they can have a look at their tails.

Jonene Taylor (8)
Lowbourne Junior School

THE WOOKEY WITCH

The Wookey Witch is indeed a sneaky creature,
No one knows she lives
Stalagmites and stalactites are the only things she eats,
As the public come a-walking,
Across the silver rocks,
The Wookey Witch wakes up from her sleep
And turns into a rock
But as the public leaves she cries 'Oh Wolf,
Oh Wolf, come here' I cry
As her small dog comes a leaping
A young child steps to the light
It gasps and screams and gives the witch a great big fright
The adults all stare round,
Their torches, flames of hell
Pick up their children,
And with a run,
Pick up some stones and pelt
The old witch takes a deep breath
And all of a sudden she melts!

Sophie Clarke (11)
Minster CE Primary School

FOOD WEEK

Monday we had meat,
It smelt like smelly feet.
Tuesday we had turkey,
It got very perky.
Wednesday we had wafers,
But nothing goes with this.
Thursday we had Sunny Delight,
We got very bright.
Friday we had fish,
We put it in a big, big dish.
Saturday we had soup,
It looked like rotten gloop.
Sunday we had salmon,
With a lot of gammon.
Now the food week is done,
That's the end of my poem.

Hayley Pearce (10)
Minster CE Primary School

MIGHTY FREEDOM

Mighty freedom
Made by God, long ago
Great, joyful, peaceful,
Like a cool green carpet,
Miles and miles of green carpet,
Makes you feel small and joyful,
Like you want to dance,
Mighty freedom
Reminds us that we are free.

Lucy Owen (10)
Minster CE Primary School

THE SILVER SNOWFLAKE

The silver snowflake,
Like a silver hand drifting from the sky,
Like a winking eye, twinkling, twinkling
There's tens, hundreds, thousands, even,
Just floating,
Like on water,
Just floating,
But this one is unusual,
This one's huge,
It is like a glistening star in the night,
Falling,
Falling to the ground,
Just lazily floating out of the sky,
Falling,
Grasping the floor,
Like a human hand,
Melting,
Melting,
Gone,
The silver snowflake.

Lewis Wilmot (10)
Minster CE Primary School

ICE

The ice is slippery like frost
As hard as brick
Smooth like paper
And melts when rain hits it
Ice goes like slushy mud
And goes back to water.

Edward Mason (11)
Minster CE Primary School

THE SIBERIAN TIGER

The Siberian tiger wandering around,
She's waiting, waiting for her food to appear,
Beware, beware the furious stripes are about to come out,
Zebra run before the tiger re-appears,
She's scuffing and gliding along the soft, thin sand,
The tiger is creeping, creeping around,

She runs faster, faster getting the sand in her eyes,
The tiger kills her prey, the zebra,
Flesh-eating animals chew away the dead body,
There's a silence, there's a drought, drought and they've
                                 just noticed it,
There is nothing to drink anymore,
The tigers are all trying to find at least something to drink, drink.
They all starve.
She drops down on the weeping and blowing sand,
Dead!

Abigail Howarth (10)
Minster CE Primary School

THE RAINBOW CLOUD

More peaceful than peace itself
Magnificent, huge, mighty
Like Heaven itself
Like a god
It makes me feel like something
Like a part of this world
The rainbow cloud
Reminds me that there can be peace.

James Quick (10)
Minster CE Primary School

UNITED IN PEACE

United in peace
The happiness poem will give you a chance
To think about the world,
Happiness, peaceful, relaxation
Well all I think is creation
Stillness, collective, happiness
Is with you,
Friends, family, relations
Will be with you
God, Jesus, people on TV
Will love you
Creatures, animals
Bugs, mammals, reptiles
Stars, moon, clouds
Will be up in the sky
Does the Holy Spirit
Run run run
Like rippling water
Life life what's the matter with that?
What happened twelve million years ago?
United in peace
United in peace
Will come to you.

Caroline Vine (10)
Minster CE Primary School

A WET PLAYTIME AT SCHOOL

Sand and water, messy paints,
Drawing, tracing, all that makes
A happy, peaceful, careful
Wet playtime at school.

Catherine Stephens (10)
Minster CE Primary School

THE SPARKLING STREAM

The sparkling stream
Trickling around the globe
Clear as glass
Looks like someone left the tap on
The sparkling stream
Bringing life
Ending death
War ends
The sparkling stream
Brings never-ending beauty to the world.

Jack Weallans (11)
Minster CE Primary School

HORSE

His name is Ernie
He's as soft as a kitten
His fur is silky
He's as fast as lightning
He's as playful as a kitten
He's as fat as fat can be
His fur is as black as midnight
He's as big as an elephant
He's as gentle as a mouse
He's as kind as a puppy
He's my favourite animal
Ernie is a horse!

Jemma Stephenson (9)
Minster CE Primary School

THE RIPPLING WATERFALL

The rippling waterfall is dazzling
It ripples over rocks and stones,
It is long, bright and colourful
It goes down slowly like something creeping,
It shines like the moon,
When it goes down it makes a splash
And steam comes out,
When the sun goes down
It sparkles like the stars,
The rippling waterfall.

Kerrie Manship (110
Minster CE Primary School

FRIGHTENING FIRE

Fire fire burning bright
In the darkness of the night
Hot, big and bright
Like the sun burning in the sky
When I'm around it I am warm inside
It is like flames against my skin
Fire fire burning bright
In the darkness of the night
It reminds us how hot fire can be.

Kelli Barrett (10)
Minster CE Primary School

THE SILVER DRAGON

The silver dragon, a remarkable sight to see
Ragefully thundering through the sky
Destructible like an army
As it rapidly destroys towns
With a single flame
The mystery about the stupendous dragon
Will never be solved
The silver dragon.

Dominic James Orchard (11)
Minster CE Primary School

BEAUTIFUL BRECON

Beautiful Brecon, beautiful sight
The lovely view is weeping to be looked at,
Peaceful wonderland, the burning sun
Houses whispering as clam glittery canals wash aside,
The sky gently sleeps away as
The waterfalls silently shout
Splish Splash! Splish Splash!

Bethany Gray (10)
Minster CE Primary School

THE GARDEN

An enjoyable peaceful place to be and play
Beautiful colours to smell and see
The wonderful wildlife to see and touch
The exotic surroundings with bright colours.

Matthew Sparks (10)
Minster CE Primary School

KIZZI THE HORSE

Kizzi is my favourite,
She's as fast as lightning,
As soft as snow,
As cute as a teddy bear,
She can be as muddy as mud,
She is my favourite horse,
I like her very much.

Danyel Creese (9)
Minster CE Primary School

LION

This lion comes from Africa
He runs as fast as lightning
He is as furry as a teddy bear
He is as fierce as a dragon
He is as cute as a kitten
But this lion comes from *Africa*!

Beth Hargreaves (8)
Minster CE Primary School

DOLPHIN

As rubbery as rubber
As gentle as snow
As soft as fur
As grey as can be.

Emma Batchelor (9)
Minster CE Primary School

EAGLE

Silent as an empty heart,
Across a distant moor,
The bird he flew the distant race,
To seek its prey in full glory.

He swiftly flies across the land,
Further than heaven could be,
Like an arrow through the clouds,
This eager bird in flight.

He swoops and cries to followers,
An eager shot again.
A bird king showing off at last
Against a crowd of crows.

If you could just imagine one
Everlasting dream,
Lonely and sad or happy and cheerful.
Silent and watchful or swift and menacing.

You too will remember the eagle
A majestic bird of the sky.

Genevieve Cox (9)
Pitton CE Primary School

UNTITLED

Mist clearing away
And colours peep through
Impressive fireworks
Set free their sparks
And coloured rain lights the sky.

The fireworks bang, babies cry
The coloured light glows in their faces
And soon cheers them up
Tea cup rides, swinging swings.

Catherine wheels roll, round and round,
Making a whistling sound,
Children smile and parents smile
Mums and dads are happy.

Stephanie Westcott (9)
Pitton CE Primary School

MY DOG

My dog's called Gareth
He's black and white
He's very playful
And awfully bright

He loves to run
And chase his ball
He runs to meet me
When I call

He can be silly
And chase our cat
A real naughty dog
'Please don't do that.'

Sometimes he has to
Go to the vet
He shakes and shivers
It makes him fret

I love him dearly
I'm sure you can tell
But when he gets dirty
He doesn't half smell!

Julie Smillie (8)
Preshute Parochial Primary School

MISS BITE'S APPETITE

We have a teacher called Miss Bite,
She has quite a large appetite.
All of the students who were bad or rude,
Would end up on her large plate of food.
One day Miss Bite felt a bit peckish,
So she ate the lunch lady with tomato relish.
The headmaster went crazy,
So she ate him with gravy.
But that wasn't enough for Miss Bite,
Miss Bite is just like a human termite,
She drank the secretary's blood with Angel Delight
But now Miss Bite needs a new place to dine
It could be your school . . . I hope it's not mine.

Matthew Bond & William Hanson (10)
Preshute Parochial Primary School

CHRISTMAS

C old white snow falling from the sky
H olly hung on people's doors
R udolph's nose is shining bright
I   vy hanging on the Christmas tree
S anta has a sack full of toys
T urkey on the table ready to eat
M ince pies being baked in the oven
A ngel's flying in the air
S tockings full of lovely toys.

Ethan Palmer (10)
Preshute Parochial Primary School

What I Spy With My Balloon

I am a balloon drifting up high,
People below can see me in the sky,
I wish they were up here with me,
Enjoying all that I can see,
Valleys, slopes, rivers and downs,
Cottages, roads, people and towns,
All living together in peace and harmony,
How I wish that would always be.

Rebecca Carter (9)
Preshute Parochial Primary School

Poetry

Poetry is fun,
Poetry can be sad,
Poetry can be happy,
Poetry can be mad,
With poetry you can do anything,
You can make it serious or silly
It doesn't matter which,
Go on have a go have a laugh
It'll be fun.

Jennifer Asherson (9)
Preshute Parochial Primary School

SMELLY MEN

The moon is shining through the night whilst
All the world is sleeping,
Suddenly one by one,
Lots of men come creeping.

Shall I tell you where they came from,
They came from beneath the drain,
Where all the sewerage runs,
And all the walls are so plain.

The stink of rotten garbage,
The smell wafts around my brain,
I hope they go home soon,
Back down the drain again.

Daniel Lowe (10)
Preshute Parochial Primary School

THE HORSE IN MY EYES

H ungry
O bedient
R eliable
S afe
E legant!

Rebecca Franczak (9)
Preshute Parochial Primary School

BOB

Today I met a man,
He told me that his name was Bob.
I said, 'What do you do for a living?'
'I'm a builder, that's my job.'

'What do you do in your job Bob?'
I asked him curiously.
'I build houses,' he answered me.
'If I do it wrong people shout furiously.'

'What else do you do in your job Bob?'
I asked him with a smile.
'I put windows in the houses,
And work for quite a while.'

'Do you do anything else in your job, Mr Bob?'
I asked the man in a curious way.
'I make the rooms look pretty,
and keep my colleagues at bay.'

'There's something else you do in your job Bob,
My mummy said to me.'
'Well people leave me the key to the house,
And give me lots of cups of tea.'

'Do you get paid a lot in your job, nice man Bob?
You must get lots and lots.'
'It depends how big the building is,
Work it out, that's also my job.'

'Is there anything else you do in your job Sir Bob?'
I asked the man in a curious way.
'I'm sorry young lady,' he said to me,
'I've had a really busy day.'

Laura Gumbley (10)
Roundstone Preparatory School

MY GOODBYE

When I said I was leaving
My good friend was hardly breathing

Then after that I began to cry
And he wouldn't even begin to sigh

My good friend thought he was dreaming
I said 'No no I am leaving'

He said without me he will be dying
I don't believe him I think he's lying

When I am gone he will be dreaming of me
And that's what he said while eating his tea

I just can't stay here, I've got to go
You just can't go!
Nooooo!

Jack Pike (10)
Roundstone Preparatory School

THE SPOOK'S HOUSE

There is a house on a hill,
It stands very, very still.
There is a sense of haunting,
It really is quite daunting.

There is a legend of a spook
Who throws around a lot of gook
The spook appears throughout the night
And causes such a terrible fright.

People say they can hear him well
Because he tends to yell and yell
He sounds like he may have a pain,
But still he cries out in vain.

Every Hallowe'en,
People say he can be seen.
But I don't think it can be true,
Do you?

Robert Comba (10)
Roundstone Preparatory School

DOGS

Most dogs are funny,
They cost lots of money,
They have cold noses,
To sniff lots of roses,
There are many colours,
Guide dogs and runners.

Some are scary,
Some are hairy,
Some are proud,
Some are loud,
They can be big or small,
But I love them all!

Alice Baker (10)
Roundstone Preparatory School

COLOURS OF THE WORLD

Red is the colour of an apple
All so juicy and red
Orange is the colour of a carrot
That rabbits use instead
Yellow is the colour of the sun
On bright sunny days
Green is the colour of the grass
So we can go out and play
Blue is the colour of a pool
So we can go swimming
Purple is the colour of the magician's cape
That he is always using
Black is the colour of the night
That makes the moon shine bright
These are the colours of the world
We should keep these colours at any price
If we keep these colours really nice
If we do it'll be better than a bowl of rice.

Sebastian Bates (11)
Roundstone Preparatory School

SPRING

Spring is coming, spring is near,
Now it's time for snow to clear,
Time for buds to reappear,
Spring is coming, spring is here.

Here comes rain for plants and seeds,
Hoping there's not many weeds,
Rain comes down in its beads,
The land below that it feeds.

Now it's time for trees to lop,
As the flowers up they pop,
Little lambs on the hop,
Gambling until they drop.

Listening to the birds that sing,
These are Christians' thoughts of spring.

Christian Cooper (10)
Roundstone Preparatory School

MY LITTLE BUNNY

My little bunny cost no money
for my mummy and my daddy
spent their money

My little bunny has a big tummy
and my mummy finds it funny

He lives in a hutch which isn't much
but my bunny loves it quite a bit

Beware of his jumping and thumping
for it might give you a scare so beware

In the night he gets a fright
when he sees a mighty fox

He likes toast the most
and carrots quite a lot

I have had him three years
and had a few tears when he disappeared.

Simon Carter (10)
Roundstone Preparatory School

The Cat

One fine sunny day
In the month of May
Sat a cat striped white and grey.
It stared into space and its face lit up
In place of a downcast yawn.

Its track could not be seen
In a patch of muddy green
And it glared with its eyes, so crystal clean
He spied a plump brown rat.
Pounce! And squashed it flat.

This furry old cat,
Known as Mat.
Belonged to a jolly old chap.
Whose name was Pat.

William Gibbs (11)
Roundstone Preparatory School

Grown-Ups

Grown-ups are bossy, bossy as can be
I don't understand it's not at all like me.
Always nagging about this and that
'Your room's a mess now clean it up,'
'Polish your shoes, brush you hair
Or you're not going anywhere!'
'Clean your bike, oil the chain,'
To turn down my music is always a shame.
Life's too short to be like this
I'd rather stay a messy kid.

Francesca Tucker (10)
Roundstone Preparatory School

COLOURS

Red is for United,
White for Leeds,
Yellow is for butter
And green is weeds.

Grey is for breeze blocks,
Orange is for a brick wall
And silver's on the signs outside
The Bristol shopping mall.

Black is for night,
Brown is for my shoe,
And blue is for the parrot
That I saw at Bristol Zoo.

Jonathan Davies (10)
Roundstone Preparatory School

KITES

On a bright summer's day
My kite flew away
It blew through the trees
In the gentle breeze

It was stuck in a tree
I asked Dad to get it for me
But he had lost his stepladder
Which made me even sadder

So I stood on his shoulders
And a pile of boulders
I reached the kite down
I wore a smile instead of a frown.

Victoria Bingham (10)
Roundstone Preparatory School

AROUND THE WORLD

Off to India off we go
Gonna see the elephants
Gonna play in the snow.
Sailing in Thailand
Gonna drink some tea
Let's build a statue, just you and me.
Playing in China
With the panda bears
Let's all climb Mount Everest.
Shopping in Sydney in Australia
Having a swim in the Great Barrier
Surfing all the waves.
Hiking in Indonesia
Looking at the plants
Seeing the monkeys doing their dance.
Walking in Saudi Arabia
Swimming in the sea
Feeding the camels, just you see
Driving in Africa
In the hot sun
Looking at the animals having good fun.
Bathing in Miami on the hot beach
Listening to the waves
Hearing the birds squeak
Going to Japan gonna go there
Went up Mount Fuji
Uh, oh, a big bear
The end of the journey
It was really good,
I hope you think this was good.

Matthew Barlow (11)
St John's Catholic Primary School, Trowbridge

EARTH

Down in the murky water,
And in the depths of the sea,
Are creatures of all sizes,
They're just like you and me!
Lions roaming in the grass,
Rabbits hopping in the straw,
And, as the sun begins to set
I turn and gaze in awe.
As the owls begin to hoot,
And the night begins to fall,
Badgers and foxes start to come out
But that isn't all.
The moon pokes her head,
Out from behind a cloud,
The owl started to hoot again,
He's getting rather loud!
I woke up in the morning,
Look out the window and see,
The sun is high up in the sky
Smiling down upon me!
Grass growing on the ground,
Some low and some high,
Little seeds in the grass,
Hoping to be trees one day in the sky!
Cows in the fields,
Grazing under trees,
Horses galloping round and round,
Their tails flapping in the breeze.

Maria Jones (11)
St John's Catholic Primary School, Trowbridge

FUN, FUN, FUN!

My kind of fun is
Hanging out with my friends,
Or driving my brother around the bend,
Going to bowling,
Or dancing to 'Rollin',
Having a laugh,
Or taking a bath,
Riding my bike,
Or taking a hike,
Going shopping,
Or doing some bopping,
Going swimming,
Or to hear my phone ringing,
Going to the park,
Before it gets dark,
Or watching Eastenders on the TV,
Is the funniest thing that could be!

Amanda Gardner (11)
St John's Catholic Primary School, Trowbridge

THE STORM AND RAIN

Here comes a scary storm,
Lightning flies through the sky,
So terribly high.
Pitter, patter, splosh,
Clouds burst into giant tears,
Drumming on the roof.

Hannah De Boorder (11)
St John's Catholic Primary School, Trowbridge

EVERYONE AROUND ME

Everyone around me
Is different to see
Some are light, some are dark.
Some have long hair, some have short.
Everyone around me is different to see
But everyone is the same to me.

Everyone around me is different to see
Some short, some tubby,
Some tall, some thin
Everyone around me
Is different to see,
But everyone is the same to me.

Ella O'Neill (10)
St John's Catholic Primary School, Trowbridge

CHOCOLATES

When I get a box of Quality Street,
There are only some I like to eat,
Caramels, mints and lots of toffee,
But never the ones that taste like coffee.
I like my sweets big and sticky,
When it comes to chocolate, I'm ever so picky,
But to find the ones I love the most,
You'd have to go from coast to coast.
My utilmate favourites are Miniature Heroes,
They're really yummy, and there are no zeros.

Jennifer Corless (11)
St John's Catholic Primary School, Trowbridge

OVER THE WORLD

Playing with the penguins
In Antarctica,
Now let's go fly on birds.
Over to Australia, off we go
Fighting with fierce snakes
With no fear.
Let's go to China
To conquer those mountains,
Let's go to see the Emperor,
Let's go to Cambodia
To do some fishing.
Now let's sail down a river,
Over to the Arctic.
Walking on the ocean
Let's go play with the polar bears,
Let's ride on the elephants,
Charge through Pakistan.
Now we'll take a trip through the desert,
Through Saudi Arabia
Into Abu Dhabi.
Let's go for a swim
Over to Africa.
Across the Sahara Desert
Let's take a dip in the Nile.
Right through Russia
Over the Rocky Mountains.
Now let's have a quick little rest.
We're back to the start in Antarctica.
I'm going home,
What about you?

Michael Barlow (10)
St John's Catholic Primary School, Trowbridge

PARENTS

Parents are so messy they're are so stressy.
They think they are cool but they are not.
They play jokes that are not funny and play like a bunny,
But they are annoying in what they do and say.

Mum's not in fashion, they think the fashion is
Like the 70's but they are always in a drag.
Dads are not funny, they smell very funny,
And have a big tummy
That's why I love them to bits!

Andrea Ling (11)
St John's Catholic Primary School, Trowbridge

CHOCOLATE

C hocolate's fun and very yummy!
H ear that rumble in my tummy!
O f course! Chocolate's what I need!
C hocolate now that it's time to feed!
O range, mint and honeycomb too!
L ater on you'll need the loo!
A ll the kinds in the world!
T ime Out, Crunchie and even Twirl!
E very time I need to eat I choose
     some chocolate, my favourite treat!

Abby Long (10)
St John's Catholic Primary School, Trowbridge

I DON'T NEED

I don't need a hole in the head
I don't need a bug in the bed
I don't need a rock on my toes
I don't need a smack on the nose

I don't need a cold in July
I don't need a punch in the eye
I don't need a very bad disease
I don't need a very strong breeze

I don't need a scratch from a cat
I don't need to slip on a mat

I don't need anything!

Daniel Welling (10)
St John's CE Primary School, Warminster

BURGERS

I like cheese burgers
I like eez burgers
I like sneeze burgers
I like leeze burgers
I like burgers
I like slime burgers
I like gross burgers
I like squeeze burgers
I like meat burgers
I like burgers.

Scott Sleeman (9)
St John's CE Primary School, Warminster

WHEN I SAW THE SHELL

When I saw the shell, I picked it up and put it to my ear
I listened carefully then I could hear
The sound was of sea animals all different kinds
There were lots of different ones but I did not mind.

Then all of a sudden a strong wind blew,
I landed on shells, all sparkly and new.
The sea colour was a cold and shimmery blue,
I started to wonder what should I do?

Then I heard a sound of a horse's hooves,
I started to shake and the ground started to move.
I felt really dizzy as I started to twirl,
I started to spin and started to swirl.

I went faster and faster until I was too fast.
Then all of a sudden, what a big blast!
I ended up on the beach with my shell.
Now isn't that a story to tell.

Kirsty Martin (10)
St John's CE Primary School, Warminster

THE BARN OWL

The barn owl flies in a cloud of grey,
Searching quietly for its prey,
Out a mouse creeps, it sees the owl
And makes a frightened squeak.
The barn owl swoops,
And the mouse scampered away.

Kelly McGrath (10)
St John's CE Primary School, Warminster

UNICORN

My unicorn was eating some grass today
And very strangely started to say,

'There's a spot on my back
My horn has gone black,
My tongue is yellow
My tummy feels like Jell-O!'

I was amazed and ran to tell,
My dad came out and started to yell
'You silly girl! There's nothing here!'
There came from my eye a sad, sad tear.

'There was! I heard it, did you?'
'There was! I heard it!' My unicorn said too.

Jade Dewey (10)
St John's CE Primary School, Warminster

FOOD

Food is yummy,

Food is scrummy.

Food is nice, just like rice.

I like chips and I like trout,
But I'll tell you now I don't like sprouts.

Ribs are red and peas are green
So when I eat my hands are clean.

Stephanie Power (11)
St John's CE Primary School, Warminster

FOOD

Food can be crunchy,
Food can be sweet,
Food can be a perfect treat,

A crunch apple,
A juicy pear,
A bag of sweets for all to share,

Spaghetti hoops from a tin,
Brussel sprouts, yuk, in the bin!

Chips and nuggets are easy to make,
For afters always cake.

Some foods we love
Some foods we loathe,
At the end of the day they make us grow.

Gemma Pickin (9)
St John's CE Primary School, Warminster

THE GHOST FROM OLD AGES

There once was a ghost
who sat on a post,
and asked the way to Norwich.
He went by the south,
and scolded his mouth,
with cold peas and
hot porridge.

Natalie Alexander (9)
St John's CE Primary School, Warminster

MY OWNER

She says I'm a golden retriever
I'll always love and adore her
I waggle my tail then wiggle my ears,
And cuddle her when she's in tears

She can't believe I'm growing so fast
But, really thinks I'm going to last.
She takes me for walks on a cold winter's day,
And wherever we go she'll know the way.

She knows I love her very much,
And that we'll never ever lose touch.
We never want to stay out long,
And when we get home we sing a song.

I lie under the table while she's having her tea,
Then she leaves all the leftovers just for me.
I gobble it up very fast
Then my pudding comes at last.

For me she throws my squeaky toy,
And then she shouts 'fetch it boy'.
Then with her bit of pocket money,
She buys me something very yummy.

She says she'll take me for a walky
Or I'll get a little porky.
I sometimes help people pick her up from school,
Then when we get home I run around like a fool.

Victoria Gill (11)
St John's CE Primary School, Warminster

THE OLD MAN

Though that door is a cat,
It's rather pretty, but rather fat,
Because all day it stays by the mat,
Poor old, poor old pussy cat.

Through that door is a man
I think his name might be Stan
But there again it might be Dan
Whatever his name he's a nice old man.

Stefan Burt (10)
St John's CE Primary School, Warminster

THE MOLE

A snuff and a sniff as he looked at a cliff,
With six fat toes and small pink nose,
The mole digs eating worms as he goes.

Katie Mae Symes (9)
St John's CE Primary School, Warminster

FALLING LEAVES

As the bitter wind blows
Past the trees
The leaves hand helplessly
To their branches
When they get too tired
And they can go no more
Twirling, whirling, fluttering,
They fall to the ground
Dying in quiet corners.

Lisa Edens (9)
St Thomas À Becket CE Primary School, Salisbury

BUBBLE, SPLASH, BUBBLE

I started off as marshy land
Up in the Welsh mountains
Bubble, splash, bubble,
I sprinkle down the mountains
Starting a trickling stream.

As I drift down a narrow valley
My strength builds up,
Suddenly, I speed up,
And get thrown over the horizon
I'm thundering over the brow
Bubble, splash, bubble!

As I fall down,
I see the rocks beneath me
I splush and gush and then I crash
Into the foam below me
I splutter over the boulders
Reaching for freedom
Bubble, spash, bubble.

I start to gently slow down
I tear away the bank beside me
And start to meander
Pushing pebbles with me
As I get wider
I drop them on my bed
Bubble, splash, bubble.

As I tear away the landscape
I form little cliffs
And channel my way through
Sparkling in the sunlight
The fisherman's net slaps my surface
Bubble, splash, bubble.

I can taste the salt of the sea!
I can see fish and crabs,
My journey is complete now;
I meet my friend at last,
Bubble, splash, bubble.

Colin Coleman & Adam Baker (10)
St Thomas À Becket CE Primary School, Salisbury

THE RIVER

Gliding, sliding, dividing,
With a rush and a gush and a plush
As I fall.
I brawl
I crawl
A splashing crashing tide
I flow in a gush, plush, splash,
Bubbling, troubling and doubling
I munch through the rocks

My trip is nearly over,
I have travelled far;
As long as I keep on
Gushing and plushing
And creeping over rocks;
I will enter the sea;
My mother and father greet me
They welcome me to the open
Bubble and splash,
I am now in the ocean.

Douglas Clifton (8)
St Thomas À Becket CE Primary School, Salisbury

PUSHING BOULDERS DOWN

Bubble, bubble goes the water,
Trickle, trickle from the source,
Splash, splash goes the tiny stream,
Crunching and munching the earth away,
Lifting pebbles and boulders
And crushing them
Tumbling and crumbling
Down the waterfall
And pushing boulders down
Curling, twisting and rounding
Through the meanders;
The river slows down
And drops its load
It gets eaten up by the sea.

Matthew Charlton (9)
St Thomas À Becket CE Primary School, Salisbury

CONKERS AND . . . BLACKBERRIES

Conkers bright and brown
Sticks and stones
Break my shell
Until I am black and blue,
Spiky and prickly
Delight of fighting boys.

I'll cling to your dress
Scratch your legs
Stain your hands
What a disgrace!

Black and juicy for you to pick
Bright and wild
I hang from the trees
Jam . . .
Glory and praise
Your work is well repaid.

Kate Young (11)
St Thomas À Becket CE Primary School, Salisbury

I Am A River

I started as a little stream
Rushing in the breeze
As I move I carry pebbles and rocks away
I can't wait
It's going to be great
I am going to the sea
I'm going to be free
I am getting wider and wider
At first I was small
And couldn't float anything at all
But later as I journey on
I'm large enough to float a swan
I really do know as I flow along
That fishermen love me
Deer come to drink from me
Small rivers join onto me
As I flow to the sea
Now my journey's ended
I have reached the sea.

Tess Carter & Tania Charlton (7)
St Thomas À Becket CE Primary School, Salisbury

A RIVER'S JOURNEY

Silently sighing down the mountain
She knows that she is only a baby and that
In the misty fog it will be hard to find her way
To her mother, the sea
Where she will be taken care of
Forever more.

She is halfway through her journey
Now, and she is very excited
For she knows that her mother
Is waiting calmly for her
So excited in fact, that she begins to go quickly
And tears off bits of land.

The river is gradually getting bigger
She knows that when she is getting
Bigger and stronger she is getting
Nearer and nearer to her beautiful
Destination and becoming one with her mother.

Finally, her journey has ended and
She is swiftly flowing to the meaning of life,
her mother;
Who is smiling and waving in joy
To see her beloved daughter
As beautiful as ever, and well.

Josie Carter (8)
St Thomas À Becket CE Primary School, Salisbury

AUTUMN LEAVES

Leaves are crunchy
They flutter to the ground
Shrivelling and dying they lie
The soft breeze sweeps them up
And carries them
To corners dark and cold
Spider webs hang
Wintry, icy and frosty
Look like silken thread, I thought
The wind is blowing
The frost is flowing in the gentle, soft air
I looked up
I saw a swirl, a twirl
The leaf landed safely
And I was glad.

Joshua Baker (9)
St Thomas À Becket CE Primary School, Salisbury

DINOSAURS

Crash!
Bang!
Wallop!
Ouch!
That's what a dinosaur's all about!

Ooh!
Ah!
Crack!
What!
That dinosaur looks like he weighs a lot!

Theo Knott (7)
Sutton Veny CE Primary School

SPRING, SPRING

It is winter now,
Spring is on its way,
Soon the flowers will peep their heads out
To see the lovely day.

The sun reflects on the shimmering water,
The ducklings swim all day long,
The reeds are growing
Soon they will be tall and strong.

We love to see the lambs dancing
So merrily in the fields
They spend their life prancing
And come to see their friends

The buds on the trees
Will soon be leaves
I hope that winter does not show
Any more of its snow.

Sophie Orr (8)
Sutton Veny CE Primary School

SPRINGTIME

I was going out with friends one day
We were going to the park to play
It was such a lovely sunny day
We passed a field on the way
In which there were some lambs at play
They were jumping here,
They were jumping there,
They were jumping almost everywhere
Oh! What a lovely day to play.

Gemma Sheppard (8)
Sutton Veny CE Primary School

HOMEWORK

I hate homework. It is always terribly hard.
It's always on my worse subject.
It's never easy, it's always hard.
It's always not what I want it to be.
But I have to do it because my mum makes me.
When the teacher says there's homework to be done,
I always say, 'Not homework again.'

I love homework. It is always lovely and easy.
It's always on my best subject.
It's never hard, it's always easy.
It's always what I want it to be.
When Mum asked me to do it I say, 'I have done it already.'
When the teacher says there's homework,
I always say, 'Yes! Homework again!'

Katie Bunce (8)
Sutton Veny CE Primary School

FRED THE TED

Fred the ted sits on my bed and keeps it snug and warm.
He gives me comfort when I'm asleep.
He's my best friend when I feel sad.
He shares all my happy times as well as my bad.
He knows all my secrets and I know he won't tell a soul.
He helps me with my homework especially when I get stuck.
We may fall out sometimes but I don't care because he's my
                                                    special bear.

Sophie Arnold (9)
Sutton Veny CE Primary School

MY FIRST TIME SWIMMING

We lined up ready to get into the water
I had to wear my armbands
I slowly climbed down the steps
Into the glistening water,
It felt lovely and warm
The lady who was teaching us
Said to 'push off the wall
and to swim to the other side'.
I said, 'I don't know how'
So she told me how to swim
She said to kick my legs as hard as I could
And move my arms.
I tried to do what she said
But no matter how hard I tried
My legs would just sink!

The next time I went swimming I was excellent
My legs didn't sink
When I came home I yelled
At the top of voice, 'I did it, I did it.'
And now I can swim like a fish.

Tansy Shingleton (8)
Sutton Veny CE Primary School

MY DREAM

I have a dream,
I'll be an astronaut
And the first in my family
To walk on the moon.
And see shooting stars and
Orion the great hunter.

Louis Frank (7)
Sutton Veny CE Primary School

RAINFOREST

The rainforest is hot,
And also it rains a lot.
There are lots of birds and animals too,
More than you can see in a zoo.
Monkeys swinging through the trees,
Birds in amongst the leaves.
Beetles scurrying on the ground,
Some animals not making a sound.
Giant red ants
Chewing up the plants.
Many exotic flowers growing all around,
Beautiful colours can be found.
Tall trees with pretty leaves,
Save our rainforest
Please
Please
Please.

Verity Prior (9)
Sutton Veny CE Primary School

THE WORLD

The world is big and round
The world is full of flowers
The world is full of animals
The world is spinning every day
The flowers grow every day
The animals grow every day.

Jonathan Ashley (7)
Sutton Veny CE Primary School

WHAT IS IT?

Droopy eyes
little legs
Floppy ears
waggly tail
Long walks

Plodding around the house and stairs
Doing whatever he cares.

What is it?
A dog.

Alex Drage (9)
Sutton Veny CE Primary School

SCHOOL

School is as boring as can be
There is a teacher looking at me.
She asks me a question, I don't know what to say,
I go to the corner, it's not my day.

I come back now I feel so bad,
Everyone is looking at me I am sad.
I kick the chair and hurt my toe,
I just can't wait for the bell to go.

Sophie Hall (8)
Sutton Veny CE Primary School

BIRDS

From early in the morning to late in the evening they sing,
You would like to catch them with a string,
But they are much too fast flying.

You would like some wings to grow on you,
So you can fly instead of doing lines of LLLs
You would really like to hear something else
Than the cow go 'moo'.

Charles Chiola (9)
Sutton Veny CE Primary School

DOLPHINS

Dolphins, dolphins swimming in the sea.
Dolphins, dolphins they are as sweet as can be.
Dolphins, dolphins swimming fast,
Now all the dolphins are free at last.

Sam Marden (8)
Sutton Veny CE Primary School

WHEN I FEEL . . .

When I'm angry I feel . . .
Mad as a shark,
I'm as angry as a dog,
As if I'm going to explode,
As if I could break a house.

Jessica Chapman (8)
Upavon Primary School

WHEN I FEEL . . .

When I get angry I get as angry as a crocodile,
Or as a volcano.
When I get angry I get angry as a lion,
Or as angry as a gorilla,
When I get angry I get angry as a rhino,
Or an elephant.

When I feel happy I feel,
As happy as a pig,
Or a teddy.
When I feel happy I get as happy as a monkey,
Or a dog.
When I feel happy I feel as happy as a doll,
Or as happy as my teacher.

Matthew Jury (8)
Upavon Primary School

WHEN I FEEL . . .

When I'm angry I feel . . .
Bombed like an air raid,
Popped like a balloon,
As lumped like a wrestler,
As hot as flames in Hell,
As noisy as my dad!

When I'm happy I feel . . .
As joyful as a dolphin,
As playful as a fox,
As funny as a clown,
As light as a feather,
Like a seal in water.

Joshua Davies (8)
Upavon Primary School

WHEN I FEEL...

When I'm angry I feel . . .
As cross as a hunter missing his prey
As red as a devil
As vicious as a vampire
As hurting as a caveman's club
As dangerous as dynamite.

When I'm happy I feel . . .
As funny as a clown
As giggly as my nanny
As happy as someone who's just got a job
As jolly as someone at a birthday
As loud as a lion.

Rachel Algar (9)
Upavon Primary School

WHEN I FEEL...

I am as hot as a volcano
I am cross as a lion
I stamp like a dinosaur
I throw my picture all over
I scream like a tiger

I smile like the sun
I laugh like a little mouse
I look so shiny like the blue sky
I'm as happy as a monkey
I chuckle like a chimp.

Shanice Collinson (8)
Upavon Primary School

When I Feel . . .

When I'm angry I feel . . .
Mad as a T-Rex just going for the kill,
As cross as a stick
As cheeky as a lion.
I throw like a tennis ball just been hit by a bat.
As cross as my mum.

Sophie Lambourne (9)
Upavon Primary School

Dolphins

Dolphins swimming through the hoops,
Diving swirling through the sea,
Doing lots of twirls and loops,
And they're the only friends for me.

Sophie Guilford (9)
Upavon Primary School

A Journey Through Space

Across the enchanting carpet of gleaming stars,
I run and jump about the moon and look there's Mars!
There is a whoosh in my face,
That ponders before me a moon rock case,
Filled with jewels and a velvet lace.
This is beginning to be quite fun,
I think I'll try and visit the sun.

Hannah Bowditch (10)
West Tytherley Primary School

MY RIDE THROUGH SPACE

I've just been shot at by a gang of shooting stars.
Uh oh! Here comes Maarrrs!
I turn left at Mercury and right from the sun,
Venus watch out here I come!

It's scorching hot, what shall I do?
I know I'll check out one of Jupiter's moons.
This isn't all that bad,
I think I'll start my very own fad!

After blowing up an asteroid,
I'm aiming for something quiet.
In fact, I will head to Saturn,
To avoid that alien riot!

I will head away from Pluto -
Because it is freezing cold.
What about the boiling sun -
No, I will probably become a giant scold!

I'm going now, I'm bored of space!
Oh no! What about Neptune and Uranus,
I suddenly feel a tear start from my face.

Jodie Brannan (11)
West Tytherley Primary School

MY HEART IS YOURS

There was a man who was very smart,
And I fell for him with all my heart.
It was a very special day,
Believe it or not it was Valentine's Day!
He said 'We shall never part, a life together we shall start.'

Katie White (10)
West Tytherley Primary School

MY SPACE GUIDE

I have a space guide who was as confusing
as my science lesson but as big as a crescent moon
He was also a fool at leading me into his left and right
and as he says his other right
Last time I went into space it was his birthday
I took him as a present but I really regretted it
I will forever, but don't let him know, it's a secret
Sssshhh
Keep it between me and you

That's it for today
from space reporter 9.

Lisa Dawkins (9)
West Tytherley Primary School

WHEN SHE WENT

Me and my friend Laura were the best of friends
Sort of like double trouble
We would stick together till the end
Just me and Laura
Till Laura moved school
She was going to Bath High
It was quite hard losing your best friend
But we would stick together till the very end
That was a few years ago
After I cried and cried
That was a few years ago
And that friendship has never died.

Ellen Bishop (10)
Wingfield CE Primary School

WASHING UP

Squeak, squeak goes
the
rusty
old
tap
drip, drip
whoosh, steam
is whirling and
curling up to the ceiling.
The sink is full at last.
Pitter-patter, pitter-patter   went the
mouse that just scuttled   by. Creak
creak go the   feet of
Mum. Splash   splish in
    go the   dishes. Splish
    splash   in go the plates.
                          Splish in go
                          the knives,
                          forks and
                          spoons.

Rebecca Mumford (9)
Wingfield CE Primary School

FIRES

Orange, red and yellow
are the flames.
There's sparks and flashes,
flickers and lights.
Watching warmly with delight.
Fire burning through the night.

Jamie-Lee Campbell (10)
Wingfield CE Primary School

THE MOON

The moon is like
a desolate sandy, glistening
world. Just imagine the little
gravity, so float away in your dreams to this
desolate, sandy planet and when you've grown
up perhaps you might be as astronaut and
visit this desolate, sandy planet, this
wonderful, desolate sandy planet, this
wonderful, desolate, sandy, glistening
with no wind, this desolate
sandy planet.

Victoria (11)
Wingfield CE Primary School

THE CATHERINE WHEEL

Sparkling bright, what a wonderful sight,
Spinning left, spinning right.
Colours red, colours white,
Hissing here, hissing there.
Twirling, swirling, faster, faster
Until the glow comes to an end.
It will all go dark when the sparks have gone out,
Leaving smoke curling up to the dark sky,
Leaving behind a horrible smell.
Remembering the beautiful colours that it had!

Christina Hallett-Young (9)
Wingfield CE Primary School

UNIQUE

Earth is special and beautiful. It is
like a greeny-blue gem floating in dark, deep space.
It is covered in glistening oceans with whales and dolphins
gliding peacefully together. Groups of tiny little fish whirling,
spinning. Fresh water streams twinkling like stars on a clear night.
Elegant, tall waterfalls splashing, crashing down to shatter the
calm surface below. Scorching deserts scattered with high sand dunes.
Interesting trees rustling and swaying in the cool breeze. Fresh
leaf green rolling hills. Colourful butterflies flickering lightly
in the air. Twittering birds spreading out their wings
in the sky. Lonely icicles in bitterly cold weather
hanging from trees - people, every one is unique.
This greeny-blue gem is your home.

Mitzi Barber (10)
Wingfield CE Primary School

BIRDS

Birds are nifty things
That live everywhere.
Finding food in cut grass.
Low in the sky, fighting bumblebees.
They appear hovering and fluttering.
Tiny feathers cover their bodies.
Making nests high in oak trees.
Catching an insect very easily.

Pat Andrew Bew (8)
Wingfield CE Primary School

ANCIENT ATTIC AND COLD CELLAR

(and something's creaking . . .)
Typewriter told of the news
Toys broken and unused
Antique vase collects the dust
Letters tell of forgotten lust
Wedding gowns, dusty and worn
Photograph albums, old and torn
Up in the attic.

Down in the cellar
The musty smell fills the air
In the corner, a two-legged chair
Humid blankets on the damp floor
The old remains of a decaying door
Mechanical tools, hidden in a box
Historic and dusty mantel clocks
(and something's breathing . . .)

Stacey Louise Button (11)
Wingfield CE Primary School

UP IN THE ATTIC

Up in the attic
some damp and musty Babygros
some old photo albums from so long ago
some old dusty trophies in a brown box
bits of memorabilia from Bristol Docks
football programmes from many matches
some rusty and dusty old gate catches
(and the floorboards are creaking.)

Tom Moore (10)
Wingfield CE Primary School

RAIN POEM

Splish
splosh
whish, wash
tapping on the
windowpanes
drumming on the rooftops

g
u
r
g
l
e

d
o
w
n

t
h
e

d
r
a
i
n

then . . .
splash into the
puddle.

Harriet Mead (8)
Wingfield CE Primary School

PUDDLES

Puddles are big.
Puddles are small.
Puddles are everywhere when the rain falls.
When it rains, it rains and it never stops.
Its shimmering shape fills in the holes
and covers the lane with water.
It wets everywhere even the moles
that dig the holes in the ground.

Stephanie Button (8)
Wingfield CE Primary School

THE FOUNDRY

For the train
That yet has no brain
There's a foundry
There's no boundary
In the foundry
Comes with dangers
But workers get
Wagers every day
Even in the
Middle of May
In the end it's
Gone round the bend.

Tom Burnett (9)
Woodborough CE Primary School

FROM FOUNDRY TO TRAIN

From foundry to train
Workers in pain
The threat of the heat
Under their feet
If you're late you must pay
Your house will be gone by the end of the day
The foundry is hot
Like a cooking pot
Men in a team
Pumping the steam
A train is made of cast iron
And roars like a lion.

Tom Keen (9)
Woodborough CE Primary School

THE FOUNDRY

It would be horrible to work in a foundry making a train
Everyone would be in pain
Lots of noise, no wonder they were all boys
In this dark room they were in all in gloom
And in fear they would meet their doom
In the light of the moon
If you were late you had to pay
And lose your house at the end of the day.

Holly Amor (9)
Woodborough CE Primary School

STEAM

Steam trains have dirty coal and wet steam,
People should always work in small teams.
Hot and misty windows and a boiling boiler,
Packed with coal with big spoilers.
But maybe you shouldn't be late,
Because you might have a little debate.
The railways go on for miles and miles,
But there must be millions of dials.
From Swindon to London all very fast,
But you would never be able to say you're last.
Hot steam in your face and you would be able to pull your horn,
But when you're in the boiler room it would always be warm.

Thomas Williamson (10)
Woodborough CE Primary School

STEAM TRAINS

A loud bell starts the day
If you're late you have to pay
Hundreds of people work as a team
To make a train powered by steam

Rich people stayed on all the time
They listen as the whistle starts to whine
The trains are always very fast
So only one gets to the station last.

Alice Nutland (10)
Woodborough CE Primary School

In The Foundry

Wouldn't it be horrible stuck down in those foundry prisons,
making those dangerous trains.
No wonder everyone was in pain,
the people who worked there were hardly human at all.
No wonder there was bags of heat,
most of it bellowing under their feet.
If you were late you had to pay
and lose your shed house at the end of the day.

In this dark room, they were all in gloom,
in fear that they would meet their doom.
They would work until the pale, dusty moon,
then they would hope to get home soon.

Lydia Sargent (8)
Woodborough CE Primary School